TAVRIDA 201

SH

Introduction

Born on January 21, 1990 in the Democratic Republic of the Congo (DRC), my name is Gerard Mutabazi Amani. I was born in Uvira which is one of the deadliest city in the Eastern part of the country where people die and flee every day into neighboring countries. This was happening in the year of 1996 when my family and I left as Refugees and it is still happening in the year of 2014. Between 1996 and 2002, we lived in several Refugee Camps in several African countries, to name a few, Tanzania, Mozambique and arrived in South Africa. It is in Cape Town, South Africa where

I registered at Cornflower Primary School in grade 2 at the age of 13. Due to moving around from one Refugee Camp to another and the hardships that the family faced, we never really settled in order to attend school and focus on building the future.

Life in South Africa was indeed better than living in Refugee Camps but we were still facing many challenges such as, food, clothes, shelter, and school fees. I am the fourth born out of eight children and every day was survival. We lived by faith and constantly praying to be immigrated to Canada in Edmonton, Alberta and it finally happened in September of 2008. Before moving to Canada I was studying in grade 7 at the age of 18 and was so excited to start High School in Edmonton when I found out that the age limit for High School was 18. A program called Youth In Transition (YIT) at NorQuest College was recommended by Catholic Social Services. My big brother, John, and I made our way to NorQuest and registered in YIT program and it was the beginning of a great, fun and amazing journey. I was tested at a grade 5 reading and writing level and I knew I had a long way to go if I want to study one day at a college or university. I worked hard with great determination and transition from YIT into Academic Upgrading in May of 2010 and the long journey continued. I persevered, believed, gave all I had and graduated with High School Equivalent Education from NorQuest College in August of 2011 after having met the requirements needed to get into Business Administration program at NAIT.

While with the NorQuest program, I was part of the RBC Ambassador team and promoted the college within the community and had countless opportunities to deliver many inspirational speeches in raising funds for students support. I was also a member of the Students' Association and had the honor of represent students and be part of the decision making. I have volunteered at different events in the community and was part of the Canadian Red Cross Youth Group before joining.

Before NAIT in the Business program, I had decided to take one year off in order to refresh and also do something which I love so much, volunteering and youth missions. I joined Canada World Youth, international non-profit organization, in September of 2011 until March of 2012 on Youth Exchange program where we spent 3 months in Ottawa, Canada and 3 months in Kimende, Kenya. This was the first time I had returned to Africa since immigrating under Refugee status. It was an exciting and mixed emotional journey but I was so looking forward to the experience. When I returned to Canada in March of 2012, I joined the Royal Bank of Canada (RBC) as a Client Service Representative in May and worked until August under their Student position. I had kept the promise which I made to myself and started the Business Administration program at NAIT in September of 2012.

I am very passionate about humanitarian work and would love to see myself helping around the world. Since arriving in Canada I have volunteered within the community of Edmonton and across the country. I have had the opportunity to attend Youth Conferences in many places including in New York City at United Nations Youth Assembly and in Russia on International Youth Forum. I have been honored and blessed to travel back to Africa in Ethiopia, Kenya and Burundi and not as a Refugee, but as proud African-Canadian.

I completed my diploma in Business Admin Management Entrepreneurship at NAIT in the summer of 2014 and I'm currently pursing my BBA in Management. I am also taking online classes at Lakeland College in their International Development Certificate program. I believe education is a powerful weapon which I can use to transform the world for the benefit of all humanity. As a former Refugee from DRC, I admired so much the work of UNHCR and the many lives they do their best to change for the better. It has been a dream come true to attend Youth Assembly at the United Nations and I look forward to attending another one in February of 2015.

In the future I look forward to writing the story of my life and this first book is the beginning of beautiful things. I have had the honor to be on Radio, TV, and Newspapers throughout the years and it is great to inspire others with all that I do. Great things comes to those who are patient and work hard with great determination for the life that they aspire to live. Please enjoy this book, Tavrida 2014: Young Leaders in Action, Shaping the Future and thank you for your support.

It all started with a Facebook post from the International Network for Youth Conferences page about the Forum and a link to the official page of Tavrida International Youth Forum. I looked at the information, thought about the opportunity and sent in my application. A few days later I received a message from Tavrida organizing committee that I had been accepted and the email came with further information to complete. I continued corresponding with them and shortly after, we were working on a visa application. I kept checking the Facebook page for any further information and I found a lot of information about the Forum, location, security, and I also found the people accepted as delegates were posting there on the Facebook page. I have taken part in Youth Missions in the past and I knew that I would love Tavrida but had no idea what to expect. I was open-minded and ready for the journey. The committee was always on the finger tip of Facebook, Email, and Skype and sometimes they would even phone me. I was ready and couldn't wait for this adventure. The following book talks about the experience from Edmonton International Airport on August 7th to the very emotional closing ceremony of the Forum on August 19th. The joy, the worries, and the unanswered questions, you will find everything in this book and much more. I hope you enjoy reading as much as I enjoyed sharing.

Chapter 1: Journey to Russia, Crimea. Why?

I have never been asked 'why' so many times in my life. I came to know about the Tavrida International Youth Forum through Facebook on a page called International Network for Youth Conferences. The organization had posted about the Forum and a link to the Facebook page of Tavrida. When I read through the details on the Facebook page, I did not think much of it but saw what I liked and loved doing and so I went ahead and applied. And you know what they say, the rest is history. The Forum was scheduled for August 10-20th

When I was telling people that in August I would be going to Crimea for a Youth Forum, I could see many questions in their eyes. Some of the questions were: why would they hold it in Crimea? Are you sure of where you are going? Who is putting this together? Most of the time I would answer their questions with, "Call me crazy, but I'm going." And to the question of why they chose to hold it in Crimea, my response simply was, I don't know. With the recent events and history of Crimea, I thought it was the best place to hold an International Youth Forum. I would also explain to people that I am a Youth Advocate who is very open minded and very adventurous. Some expected more explanation of why I'm going and more information about the Forum itself. Over the years I have learned that if you want to live life to the fullest, don't think too much, but just go with the flow. In this case, the Federal Agency on Youth Affairs of the Russian Federation had communicated to all delegates that many different measures would be put in place to ensure our security. During the process of the application, the organizers were giving us all the details needed to ensure that we were comfortable and aware of where we were going. For me, I don't need to have answers to everything in order to follow my heart. At times I felt it when my heart was communicating and I put my mind on the side. With everything that had been going on with Russia and Ukraine in recent months, my heart communicated with me to just go. If I had put all the pieces together and listen to just my head, I wouldn't have gone. And we are all also very aware of the Canadian and Russian international relationship.

August 6th came around and it was time to get ready for the journey. My flight was scheduled for August 7th at 7:15am. I decided not to sleep on August 6th and used the night to do some cleaning and getting ready for the journey. Two of my friends and brothers, Tresor and Eto'o, arrived at my home after 2:00am because they were going to drive me to the airport. I finished getting ready, we watched a bit of TV and left for the airport after 3:00am. I checked in my baggage, got my tickets and said farewell to my friends.

For some reasons, I was worried about whether the US Customs would allow me to pass through to the United States. Over here in Canada we have US Customs and Boarder Protection at the International Airports if you are flying to the US. Before reaching the US soil you have to go through US Customs in Canada. My flight was scheduled for Newark and from JFK airport to Moscow. Between Newark and JFK I had to take ground transportation. So I was on the US Customs line at Edmonton International Airport. It was then my turn to see the Customs Officer. I stepped forward and gave him my passport with greetings. He asked me where I was going and I simply responded that I was going to Russia in Crimea. He almost looked as if he took a step backward.

The Officer asked what I was going to do in Crimea. I told him I was going for an International Youth Forum which was being put together by the Youth Affairs of the Russian Federation. Just like many before him, he also asked why the Forum was being held in Crimea. I responded by saying that I was not sure why they chose Crimea. Questions after questions, after questions kept on coming. He asked, "Are you sure of where you going, will you be safe?" I replied and said "Yes I'm sure of where I am going. I am a Youth Advocate and love to experience new things and challenging myself." The Officer kept on looking at me, my passport, and into his computer system. I was very worried about whether he would allow me to pass through the US with the recent situation between

Russian and Ukraine and the US and their relations. After a long pause, the officer said, "Sir due to recent events in Crimea, please come with me." And this is when my worry increased, but in my heart I was praying for them to allow me through. I kept my calm and answered the questions accordingly and was acting very confident meanwhile I was worried to death. The line was long, I had spent more than 5 minutes being interrogated, and yet I was taken into a room for further questions. I had printed all the papers about the Forum and my invitation letter, but still it was not enough.

In the room I also founded a couple waiting. I laid back on a chair, closed my eyes, and thoughts started running through my head. I was called to the front desk by a different Customs Officer. He asked me some of the same questions and I politely responded accordingly. The previous Officer had passed on my passport and papers to the officer who was now further interrogating me. My luggage was already checked in and when I saw it in front of me, my heart started beating and my worry increased. I started to wish that my layover could have been somewhere else beside the US. The Officer asked me to open my luggage. Before going through it he asked me what was in my luggage and I told him. He was wearing gloves on his hands and he searched through my bag. I don't know what he was looking for but after not finding it, he locked my bag and returned it for check in. During this process, I was calm and polite like never before. At last he put a US stamp in my passport and I was free TO GO!!! I was happy, I looked up to the ceiling and thanked God. 7:15am came and the flight was on route to Newark, New Jersey. We landed after 12pm and I went to get my luggage. I spent over an hour making a decision of what kind of transportation to take to JFK for my flight to Moscow.

    I finally decided to just pay $32 for a car and was on my way. There was traffic on the way to JFK and I started to worry that I would miss my flight. I was very hungry and sleepy because I had not slept the night before. At times the car was not moving at all because of traffic and I kept on asking what time it was. My flight was supposed to leave at 7pm and I arrived at the airport 6:30pm. I had given up hope and thought there was no way I was going to make this flight. Despite my giving up hope, I was still praying within my heart to make the flight and saying to myself that I cannot afford to miss this flight. I got out of the car with my bag and ran quickly to Russian Airlines. I was told that the gates had already closed. I felt as if the world had come down and I was wondering what to do next. While I was standing and speaking with the airline people, a couple arrived who were also late for the same flight. They said the reason was also because of traffic. Now I was glad to not be alone and we asked if we could be let in. The lady who was helping us phoned the airplane to see if we could still be let through. After hanging up, she turned to us and said, "You can go through, but your luggage will have to stay and will be sent tomorrow." With big similes on our faces the three of us said, no problem, with excitement. We left our bags and ran to check in as quickly as possible. We found people were still getting onto the flight and there was a long line. I took a deep breath and thanked God for everything. A Few minutes went by and we were all checked in and on the airplane.

  We landed in Moscow at Sheremetyevo International Airport around 12:40pm. The flight was great with nice Russian food, movies, and great service. Before everyone was allowed out of the flight I heard "Amani Gerard" on the intercom but speaking in Russian. I didn't know why they had called my name. I asked the person next to me whether the person being called should go somewhere. He responded and said "Yes, go see the captain." Everyone was asked to stay seated while I was led to front of the airplane. One attendant lady asked for my passport and then asked me when I was last in Africa. I told them in June of this year, but I was in East Africa. She said okay and handed me my passport back. Everyone was then allowed to leave the flight.

    I proceed through the checkout. I handed my passport to the Officer and she took about 5 minutes looking back and forth at me, my passport, and asked me to sign three times on a piece of paper. On my passport I have an Afro and I have changed, but not much. The Officer called another lady to come and take a look. Throughout the over 5 minutes of me standing there and them verifying me, I did not communicate with them because I did not know any Russian, but I was trying to smile with all my worries. They took so long that I started to get worried and think maybe they won't let me through or they might take forever. After a few more minutes the two ladies came to a decision and they stamped my passport and allowed me through. I proceed to checkout, but before exiting, I registered that I left my luggage at JFK with Russian Airlines and was told that it will be sent tomorrow on the next flight. I filled out some papers which were in English, thank God. I was now ready to exit, FINALLY. I stepped outside to the welcoming and waiting area, looked at the people who had names on the card, and I saw a tall and beautiful lady holding my name. I walked up to her and said, "Hi, I'm Gerard." She said her name was Sasha and that there were three other guys from Serbia already waiting at the Airport for me.

After a long journey of questions, traffic, and worries, I could finally relax because I have arrived. We passed by a place to exchange money within the airport and joined the three guys. We were introduced to each other and together we started the journey to the hotel where the rest of the Delegates were to meet. We took the first train which was over 30 minutes which was called the airport express. After that we took the metro deep underground. The train was moving very fast and people were not even able to make conversation because of the underground noise and opened windows. At times, I was taking a moment to close my eyes and think back on the journey and think of how I was really in Russia for the first time. I was very grateful and you could see nothing but smiles on my face. The worries had finally gone and no one here could ask me why I was going to Crimea or the many other questions which I was not able to answer. I choose to go with my heart most of the time and I am always keen to challenge the unknown and live life to the fullest. At the end of the day, that is what makes life worthwhile.

We spent over an hour from the airport to hotel. Sasha was the one leading us and we had no idea where we were going. All I had with me was the clothes I was wearing, which I had been wearing for the past 2 days. I also had my backpack. We arrived at the hotel in the afternoon and were very tired, but because of my enthusiasms, I was alive like never before. It had not been easy getting here and not everything comes easy in life. I put all the questions, voices, and unknown questions behind me and followed my heart which led me to Moscow, Russia for the first time and soon to Crimea. I was honored, humbled, and grateful to the Most High and all those who continue to support me. I was so excited and could not wait to meet my fellow delegates and go to Crimea with an open mind. All is can say is, LET THE JOURNEY BEGIN.

Chapter 2: Tavrida International Youth Forum: This Is It

The excitements at the hotel proceeded as many more Delegates began checking in. I met with the organizing team and was offered a room on the second floor of the hotel. I introduced myself to a gentleman named Macpherson, who was one of the delegates. He was originally from Zambia but has been studying medicine in Russia for the past few years and was about to finish. I told him that I was born in the Democratic Republic of Congo, but I was coming from Canada. Around 5pm the delegates were invited to go for food in a different room. I looked at the food and asked Macpherson, "Is this supper?" He responded "Yes, that's the food." Our supper was pieces of bread, which we helped ourselves to, something that looked like porridge and tea. After a long journey from Canada, the worries, and being very tired, what I needed was real food because I was very hungry, but I had no choice but to eat what was in front of me, and be grateful to have it. After supper I went into my room and went on the internet for a while. I used this opportunity to take a shower, but could not change my clothes because my luggage was hopefully coming tomorrow.

After refreshing I went back downstairs where more delegates were arriving and being checked into their rooms until tomorrow when we were all leaving for Crimea. It was now after 6pm when all arrived delegates were asked to gather outside for a tour of the Moscow Red Square. More delegates were still arriving when we left and so we were only over a dozen on the tour. The organizing team led us to the metro station and we took the train to the Red Square. A gentleman named Nickolas, from the organizing team, was giving us a short history of the places we passed. Being on this tour now felt like I had arrived in Moscow and it was an awesome feeling. We passed on the bridge over the Moskva River and soon reached the Red Square. It looked so beautiful with a great view of buildings and the Square looked very busy with a lot of people taking pictures. For me it always brings joy to my heart to be among the company of Youth Delegates from around the world. Getting young people together is a great way to go about having a better world because we are the present and the future. Thailand, Serbia, Namibia, Zambia, Morocco, Ecuador, Mexico, Russia and Canada were just some of the delegates present at the tour, with many back at the hotel.

It is always an honour and pleasure to meet young people from all corners of the world. I love learning about people's cultures, languages, and how things operate in their respective nations. We went around Red Square and took pictures. It was now getting dark and after 9pm some people went back to the hotel with part of the organizing team. Some of us decided to stay and explore more with other members of the organizing team. We went around and stopped for something to eat because many of us were so hungry. For me personally, there was no way I would go to bed with only the food I ate at the hotel after such a long journey. We went into a place where you chose what you wanted, put the food on the plate and the price was dependant of the weight of the food. We put some meatballs, rice, spaghetti, and some tomato sauce to go with all that. Oh and I also got a bottle of water. All that was 700 Rubles which comes to about 20 Canadian dollars. I ate until I was full and decided to take the remaining food to go because I didn't want to waste. Some of the delegates had bought pizza. My stomach was now full and I felt great with a big smile on my face. I had now arrived in Russia!!!! After 11pm we decided to start heading back to the hotel. As usual the journey back to hotel was long and I felt very sleepy. My eyes were very heavy and shutting down.

When we arrived back at the hotel, we found many more delegates already checked in and some were just relaxing on the main floor. I greeted a gentleman from Syria, brothers from Nigeria and a sister from Kenya among others. So far the African delegates had all been living in Russia and I had yet to see one from directly from the Motherland. During my conversation with the fellow

African delegates we talked about how it would be very hard for Africans to come directly from Africa for the Forum. We talked about how challenging it can be for them to get visas, and the recent situation, Ebola, in West Africa. We were having a conversation like we had known each other for a long time. You could see the joy in everyone's eyes with laugher and stories whether about themselves or what's going on around the world. I also shared my worries while with US Customs and the many questions before landing in Moscow. It was a miracle that I was even present because at one point I thought I had even missed my flight.

My Nigerian brothers were very hungry and so I gave them the little food that I had packed. I am not sure if it helped much though. My tiredness was now getting to me, with my eyes becoming very heavy so I decided to head to my room. I had communicated with fellow delegates that I will be back shortly but I didn't go back downstairs. I felt very sleepy while I was checking my email and Facebook and put my laptop aside for some rest. At this moment I was feeling half dead. I had not slept in the past two days, but my excitement was lying to me and keeping me awake.

The next morning, August 9th, I was up by 9am. Even though I was tired, I had woken up early because I was still on a different time zone. I decided to stay in bed for a while and around 10am, Egor, one of the organizing team member, made an announcement on the intercom for delegates to go for breakfast if they had yet to do so. I went for breakfast with my roommate, who was from Syria. More delegates had arrived during the morning and met some of them throughout breakfast. Our breakfast was one egg, tea, bread, and some porridge. This was okay for breakfast and I did not worry like the last night when we had supper.

After I finished breakfast I was called by a member of the organizing team to get my documents and head to the airport to check for my luggage. The flight from JFK was to arrive at Sheremetyevo airport before 1pm, like yesterday. I went into my room and gathered the papers which I had filled out yesterday to register my baggage and I also took my passport. I was escorted by a young lady, Sasha. She was a different Sasha than before, not the one who picked me up from the airport upon arrival, but she was also a volunteer with the organizing team. We left the hotel around

11am and took the long journey back to the airport. After taking two metros, we soon arrived at an express train station which went straight to the airport. I had paid for myself from the hotel until we reached the station, but did not have enough cash to catch the express train to the airport. Yesterday I had exchanged $50 and when I checked in my wallet, I did not have enough money for the ticket. The one way ticket was 400 Rubles and I tried to use my Visa card, but the machine rejected it. Sasha paid for me and I later paid her back when I exchanged more money. Sasha informed me that Nika, another volunteer, would be waiting for me on the other side because she had to go somewhere. I had thought that Sasha would escort me straight to the airport, get my bag, and we would come back together. She told me that the train would not stop until it reached its final destination, the airport.

 The train was already waiting there and so I got in. It was quite a long ride of over 30 minutes and I was sleepy during the way. When the train came to a full and complete stop, I exited and looked around for a lady waiting for me. I knew her name was Nika, but did not know what she looked like and so I had another thing to figure out. Just when I was about to exit the train station, I looked to my right and saw a lady standing and holding papers. The Tavrida International Youth Forum sign was not visible but I walked up to her and it turned out she was Nika. She told me that Elena, a delegate from Lithuania, had just arrived and was waiting for us. I was introduce to Elena and she continued waiting with us while Nika and I went to get my bag. We spent over 5 minutes going in different directions and finding the right place to ask if my bag had arrived.

After asking a number of people we finally located the place where all luggage arrives if it is left by owners or misplaced. Nika communicated with the lady in Russian and she asked me to provide the papers which I had filled out yesterday and my passport. The lady in charge then allowed us to search for my bag among many other bags. Some of them had arrived today while others had been there for a while. The room was almost full with bags of all kind. I saw a bag which looked like mine and yes indeed it was my bag. I was filled with joy that I could finally change out of these clothes I have been wearing for two days. I took the bag and we approached the lady to tell her that it was mine. She finished her paper work, I signed and we were out. Elena was patiently waiting for us and Nika had started to get worried because we took so long. Elena and I exchanged our currencies for some Rubles and we went to take the express train for a journey back to the hotel. We arrived at the hotel and some delegates had already gone for a zoo tour. It was something that I was looking forward to, but was unable to make it because of my bag. The hotel was looking more alive with many delegates. I went into my room for a shower, changed my clothes and joined the others for supper.

    Evening came and we were asked to gather our luggage and stay outside with it to start our journey to Crimea. All delegates brought their luggage outside and we waited while we were put into teams for our bus ride to the airport. Nickolas was calling out the names together with our respective countries. You could hear countries such as Egypt, Syria, Palestine, China, India, Tanzania, Serbia, Vietnam, Pakistan, US, Nigeria, Canada, Namibia, and many more. If world leaders could see what was happening at this moment, maybe the world would be a better place. We came from different corners of the world and from different background, but one thing unites us all, our love for a better and more loving world. I was ready to spend the next ten days with these delegates in the hopes of learning and connecting with each other during our stay. The names were called, teams were formed, and we headed for the buses. The excitement was mounting and you could see the big smiles on people's faces ready for the long journey. There are three international airports in Moscow and our flight to Crimea was to take off at Sheremetyevo, the airport which I landed at. The journey to the airport was over 2 hours long and we arrived after 8pm. We all stayed in our teams as we went to check in our luggage and get tickets. All was set and ready to go.

 We checked in through security and the teams were divided between two gates. We had almost an hour to chat and get to know some of the delegates before we boarded the flight. The place we were standing came alive with the laugher of young people about stories from different walks of life. We laughed like crazy and took a lot of pictures while some of the passengers were looking at us. The time came to board the flight and it felt like our own private jet. The laugher and fun continued in the flight and slowly people started to fall asleep. Many of us had traveled very far with little sleep in the past two days. We landed in Simferopol, the capital city of Crimea, after 2am on August 10th. We got off the flight and the team made sure everyone was accounted for by calling us by names and putting us into new teams which we would be together for our stay. We took our luggage and after everyone was put into teams, then it was time for another long bus ride. Teams were formed with delegates of 15 up to 20 and there were 7 teams. I was on team lucky number 7. We gathered our belongings and got into buses. The journey to Sevastopol and into the camp ground was 2 hours long.

Sevastopol is the largest city in Crimea with a rich Russian history of many wars fought. The bus was very quiet and everyone was deep into sleep when we were woken up around 4am as we had arrived. Our camp was located at Kachin Bay next to the Black Sea. We got off the buses and we stood in line to be checked in with our passports, more security check, and be handed our badges. The badges had our first and last names with our photo ID. The journey from Moscow to Sevastopol was very long, but despite our sleepless days and people being tired, no one was in a sleepy mood. Our excitements was overpowering our need to sleep. The camp ground was full of many small tents which would be our homes for the next 10 days. Now the real journey had begun. Even though I could not answered many questions before leaving Canada, I was at a place where my heart felt at peace me and I was prepared for any outcome. As a proud Youth Advocate and Humanitarian, I want to live life to the fullest and challenge the perceptions. Before the tensions between Ukraine and Russia, I had never heard about Crimea in my life and yet here I was. Right on the ground to witness, learn, and just enjoy my time with fellow youths.

Chapter 3: Ready. Set. GO!!!

We completed the check-in process into camp and were led to our leaders. All teams had two leaders and the leaders were to take care of the delegates until the Forum was over. One of the leaders of Team 7 was Denys, from Sevastopol. Our other leader for the stay was Nika, the lady who helped me get my bag from the airport. Learning that she would be part of Team 7 was great because I was very grateful to her for the trouble of going up and down in search of my bag. Denys and Nika were now in charge of the team and we all sat for some camp rules. Rules such as no open fire, no smoking on camp ground, no wandering around after curfew and many more were read out loud.

The members of the team then introduced themselves and stating the country being represented. Remember Elena, from Lithuania? She was part of Team 7. Other delegates part of Team 7 were from Nigeria, India, Russia, Japan, Algeria, Kyrgyzstan, Ecuador, Canada, Palestine, Pakistan, Indonesia, Latvia, Kurdistan, China, Namibia, and later someone from Ukraine joined us. There were about 17 delegates from Team 7 and no two people were from the same country. This was very interesting and we all observed this aspect of the awesome and unique team that had been put together.

Paul, a gentleman from Nigeria, and myself shared a tent and he was the best roommate I ever had. Instead of sleeping, we decided to walk around and inspect the campground. We were really inspecting but among our findings, we noted that the washrooms were not labelled whether male or female and Paul decided to do something about it. With me being his assistant, we walked around in search of something which we could use to label the washrooms. We told some of our superiors about the situation and soon we were directed to where we could find paint and a brush. Paul finally was able to label the washrooms with the paint. The interesting part is that after a few days, the washrooms were labeled by those in charge. I guess they might have been more complaints and maybe the paint was not clear enough. The morning was very hot and the tents were very heated so that I did not think people could survive inside. This first day of camp was very relaxing because it was too hot to even do anything. The heat made me very weak and I could also see the expressions of fellow delegates that they also could not handle this kind of heat. We were allowed to go for a swim and this allowed for our continuous introduction to each other and also to learn more about what we do. It was dinner time in the evening, but I was no fan of what we had. It was a very light dinner of bread, soup and something else, not much different from the one we had in Moscow.

Night time came and with it, entertainments. The entertainment place was held at the same grounds where we held our Forums and about a 10 minute walk from the actual campground. The sun had gone down and we danced, danced, and danced like there was no tomorrow. You could see the joy on people's faces and I felt so great to be in the company of young people for the next week days. The music finished around 00:00 and it was nap time and we headed back to the campground. I had showered but still was not sleeping. We had wireless internet at the camp and so I used the internet and finally decided to rest. I had not slept well for the past few days because of the long journey, time change, and the excitements of being around fellow passionate youths for a better world. The first day of camp was now in the history books and I was ready for whatever laid ahead.

The morning of August 11th started with a wakeup by our leader and followed with some exercises. There was a place where people danced for exercise and a DJ was leading the way. I have never done exercise to dancing music and this felt quite great. After the exercise I took a shower and we then had breakfast. Everyone was set and ready for the Forums to begin. Our first presentation was on Russia history where the presenter talked about Russia through different phases of war. A lady from Brazil, Caroline, had done the introduction with a loud and exciting welcome to everybody. Caroline then explained a little bit about herself being from Brazil but spent many years in Russia, her travels, volunteering and being part of AIESEC in Russia and Brazil. Sounds like she has had quite an adventurous life living across borders and being involved with youth missions. She's for sure among the people that I consider inspiring.

It was now lunch time and the afternoon session was with a VIP guest, the deputy minister of Education of the Russian Federation. He took questions from the crowd, talked about Russian education system and sponsorship opportunities for International Students. This was a very educational session. It was now dinner time and we were allowed to go swimming after that. This evening's entertainment was officially the opening ceremony of Tavrida International Youth Forum. It was filled with excitements, the Russian anthem was played, the beauty of Russia was showcased on the big screens and we even received personal greetings and welcoming by the Russian President, Vladimir Putin, through one of his delegates. Even though I did not understand the language, the Russian National Anthem sounded so awesome. The National Anthem and a song called Tavrida by Maria Bulavina became our Anthems for the rest of the camp. Every morning you would hear the beautiful voice of Maria while still sleeping. Among all the music that was played at the Forum, I fell in love with those two Anthems and every time they would come on, I was at peace. We concluded the night of August 11th full of energy, excitements and not feeling sleepy at all. The entertainment finished after 23:00 and I headed for sleep after taking a shower. The morning of August 12th came, we went for exercise as usual and had shower. Some people would skip the exercise session and get those few extra minutes of sleep before morning session begins.

After breakfast our morning session was about Russia and its world relations, and international organizations such as World Bank, IMF, UN and BRICS. The conversation was led by a Professor from a university within Russia. We had a very heated debate about the role of the UN Security Council and I could see the passion in people's eyes and hear from their voices. I realized that fellow delegates were ready for change within the UN Security Council in order to include the representation of other continents. The Professor however noted that the UN is the only world powerful governing body which we have and we cannot afford to bring down the whole system. It was now lunch time and after that we had our afternoon session. Our VIP guest this time was the Foreign Minister of the Russian Federation. He spoke about current issues such as Crimea. I remember asking him a question along the lines of, "In the global community that we're living in, Western nations are putting sanctions on Russia, how will Russia survive?" He responded by saying that Russia was a very big country with lot of resources and the question is not about surviving because the sanctions are not affecting the country. After the VIP guest, we gathered at the campground and got ready for our first tour. Buses were waiting for us outside the camp together with a traffic police escort.

Each bus had a tour guide and the buses were big and looked so nice and very pleasant to ride in. I could see the excitement among fellow delegates during the tour. We visited the 35th Battery in Sevastopol and the history of wars that Russians battled was explained to us. We learned about the fight over Crimea between Russia and other European nations and how Russia became victorious. I felt a part of history and I was grateful to be where I was at this very moment learning with fellow youths. We arrived at the camp very late from the excursion and I was feeling very tired so I just went straight to sleep.

The morning session for August 13th was very lively and exciting because it was all about staying active and we were visited by the Minister of Health and Sport. He spoke about being involve with the recent Olympics of Sochi 2014 and encouraging young people to stay active. We even did some jumping exercises and other fun engagements. After this, some gentleman took over talking about business opportunities. After lunch our VIP guest was a Russia director of one of the movies which was showcased and he took questions from the audience about his work directing and promoting Russian movies.

The movie had subtitles for English speakers, but I couldn't even see the subtitles because I was sitting too far away and people were blocking me. I just sat there, while sometimes trying to rise my head to see the subtitles but eventually I just gave up. I decided to close my eyes while the movie was playing because I was very sleepy and my eyes were very heavy. The movie was finally over and it was dinner time. After dinner I made the decision to not go for the evening entertainment because my voice was very low and I could not afford to shout and scream. I wanted to save my voice for next day's entertainment and let it get back to normal as I stop yelling. I stayed in the tent on the internet and I could hear the music and screams coming from the entertainment grounds. At times I wanted to get out of the tent and just go and enjoy the fun but stayed in the tent until I was ready to sleep.

The morning of August 14th saw more Russian and Crimean history with different fighters being highlighted. I love history but I had never learned so much all at once and the speaker was being translated into English right on the stage. Some other speakers who were communicating in Russian, we had a lady who would translate from inside of a small room and we were offered earpiece in exchange for our badges. We had to have our badges with us at all times and without them we were not allowed to move around. I remember there was this one morning when one of the delegate was spotted by the security without his badge on, he was told to go back and get it. This is how important those badges were and I made sure that I had mine on every time before I left the tent. This is how well the Forum was organized with the best security possible for the safety of everyone. After lunch our VIP guest was the Minister of Education because on the second day we were visited by his deputy. He also spoke about opportunities for International Students to stay in Russia on Government sponsorship, the language requirements, and about how that information can also be found at Russian embassies across the world. He touched on the point that those who are educated always think different from others and have better chance for the best living standard. The Minister of Education was surly among the most exciting VIP guest we had, he was full of energy. After the session we were given few minutes to gather at the buses waiting for us for another moving excursion filled with fun and learning.

I communicated with a Russian Professor called Vladimir who studied in Canada at SAIT in Calgary back in the day. I informed him that I am a Business Student at NAIT in Edmonton taking Management and he seemed very pleased to connect with me. He gave me his information and I had to run and join the others at the buses. This excursion went on to be among the most memorable outings filled with lot of pictures, sightseeing, even dancing and some worries. We visited once again Sevastopol and this time it was more into the core of the city. We boarded the previously mentioned big and beautiful buses with police escort and the same tour guides. It felt as if we were diplomats. In some ways, yes, we were indeed young and promising diplomats ready to take on the world. The name of our tour guide was Natasha and she would explain to us through the intercom some of the important facts of where we were going.

Whenever we got off the buses, you could see many of the locals setting eyes on us as if to say, "Who are these people?" Some locals were even asking for pictures with us. There were some women who had beautiful dresses on and holding flowers and you would pay to take picture with them. Other people had lovely birds which they put on you for a small payment to take pictures. These were nice and quick ways to make a living from the tourists coming for sightseeing. At first I did not know that one had to pay in order to take a picture and something happened. I saw Julius, a delegate from Namibia, holding two birds and I ran to him and we started taking pictures. It seemed like a fun and enjoyable moment and suddenly the owner of the birds started asking for money. I looked confused and did not know what was going on until it was explained to me that one has to pay in order to take pictures. Julius told me that the gentleman had agreed without payment, but now he had changed. I did not have much money on me and because I had no idea of the outcomes, I decided to walk away and left Julius dealing with the owner of the birds. Afterward I reconnected with Julius and he explained to me that he gave him a small amount and said that the bird owner was very tricky.

 We continued with our excursion and learned more about Crimean history, saw the beautiful Black Sea from a different side and then joined in the entertainments put together by the locals. There were some musicians playing for people to donate and Jerry, a delegate from Nigeria, joined in the fun when he took over the piano. And suddenly many of the delegates joined in and some started dancing to the music. The gentlemen playing were very awesome and Jerry was just marvellous and brought delights from all people who were present and the locals loved him so very much. At times it is very hard to explain the excitements, but you had to be there to understand and feel the emotions of people having so much fun. It was now time to meet back at the buses and head back to the campgrounds but Paridhi, a delegate from India, and Anna, from Serbia, were nowhere to be found. Everyone was seated in the buses and ready to go and the two ladies still could not be found. Our leaders asked if we had seen them and the response from all delegates was of a concerned no, we didn't know where they were. Everyone spent the next minutes worrying and thinking where they could be as we patiently waited in the buses while some of our superiors search for them. We heard some singing happening outside the buses and quickly the delegates including myself went outside dancing and responding to loud cheering.

The fun had continued while we waited for the arrival of Paridhi and Anna when our superiors ordered everyone to get back into the buses. The ladies finally arrived and when asked where they were, they responded that they were around. They had kept everyone waiting and now we were running late when we finally headed back to the camp. Many delegates, including myself, were not happy with their actions of wandering around while they knew the meeting point and time. We arrived at the camp after 23:00 and the evening entertainment was still going on, but I decided to take a shower and relax because I had had enough fun for the day. So far Tavrida had been filled with memorable moments of learning, networking, dancing, and just being young people and of course the heat at times was leaving people very weak. If I could just stay in cold water the whole day, I would surly do that because I was sweating and not sleeping well at night due to the tent being very hot.

Sometimes when I came from the shower and got into the tent, I started sweating as if I have not even showered. The heat made the everyday walk to the learning sessions very difficult and I was just wishing to stay under a tree for the cool and fresh weather.

Chapter 4: Young Leaders in Action

August 15th was yet another beautiful, hot and blessed morning. The first line that I had wrote into my journey entry was, "The Forum has been awesome and I'm grateful to the Lord for everything." In everything I do, I give thanks, glory, and honour to the Most High for all his wonders and blessings. Life is a beautiful gift and I take everything as special as the previous. Waking up next to my brother, fellow delegate, and youth leader from Nigeria, Paul, made all the days even worthwhile. This gentleman became my best friend and we talked and gave each other advice on many things. He admired and appreciated what I brought to the Forum and it was no less the other way. We had great respect and love for each other throughout the Forum. We would talk about our previous youth missions, education, Africa, experiences, and all that we hoped to achieve. Most of the time I could be found with Paul.

Another gentleman who I was very close with was Donatus, also a delegate from Nigeria. I regarded him as a big brother, mentor, and most importantly, a friend. He did not have a camera with him and mine became his. If I did not have my camera with me, it was with my brother Donatus. Because he would take a lot of pictures, there was no point in me having it. When one of the delegates said that if I was to lose this camera and someone found it, "The person would think it belongs to him [Donatus]." This is how much love I had for him. The camera become almost his and together we also become inseparable.

We would talk about life, education, our desires for the future, and wishing nothing but the best for each other. I told him I have always had a great love for Nigeria and almost went there in May of 2014 for a Youth Conference when it was suddenly postponed. Throughout the years, my family and I have been huge fans of Nigerian movies and I learned their ways of communications.

The way I would sometimes communicate with Donatus, he would even mentioned that, "I sound just like a Nigerian." At the Forum, I respected and treated all as brothers and sisters and I became close to many of the delegates. I remember one time a brother from Palestine, Attaf, who was also part of Team 7 talked about the situation between Israel and Palestine. Even though I did not communicate much in English, I could feel his pain and desire for a better future for his people.

Attaf had mentioned that he has a documentary which he would love to share with those interested, but we never had the opportunity to watch it. Something beautiful which brought a lot of emotions happened at the Global Village on August 18th and you will have to keep reading in order to find out what happened. This is the day when everyone proudly raised their flags, some wore traditional clothing, many performed songs and traditional dances and the whole world became together as one. Look at me, I'm getting carried away with the events of August 18th, let us stay on August 15th for now.

After finishing the morning exercise, I had a shower, breakfast and was ready for the morning session. Most of the times I would walk with Paul to the sessions and if one of us was not ready, we would wait for the other. The morning session started when two ladies presented on Petrozavodsk State University in Russia and talking with International opportunities for International Students. At most of the Institutes in Russia, people have to either already be able to communicate in Russian and be willing to spend at least one year learning Russian before specializing in field of interest. After the presentation from the ladies, it was now time for Youth Leaders to be in Action.

The night before, we were given the opportunity from our superiors that if people had a topic of interests to bring forward, we would be given the platform to present and engage our fellow delegates. I believe there were six people who had brought topics forward and August 15th became very interactive, educational, and a day with youth learning from each other. I did my topic on 'Poverty among Youth and Children'. We were given 90 seconds to step in front, introduce our topics and invite others to participate. I had found some statistics about children living in poverty on the UNICEF website, I brought up the MDGs and the UN wanting more youth involvement post 2015 and invited people to come and discuss the causes and put down some solutions.

My brother Donatus had presented on 'The Threat to the Global Environment' where he talked about our actions toward climate change, the threat, and solutions moving forward. Donatus wrote a piece on this topic and you will get to read it at the end of this book. A fellow Canadian, Kayla, presented on 'Sustainable Orphanages' where she talked about how Orphanages can sustain themselves for the long run and not only depend on funding. Paridhi, who in short we would call Pari, present on 'Women Empowerment' mainly focusing on India. Fellow delegates went to whichever topic they connected more to and the room came alive. Other topics were 'The New "Iron Curtain" Between East and West' by Elena from Lithuania (Eriko from Hong Kong had joined her), 'The Necessity of a University Degree' by Yagouba from Guinea and 'Project Sustainable Maritime Territory of the Black Sea in Crimea' by Simon (USA) and Natalia (Russia). Julius did his topic on 'Slavery in the 21st Century'. We had a few minutes to discuss the respective topics, suggest possible solutions, summarize our findings, and present back to the larger group. After this a presentation on 'Global Education' was done by three delegates from the US, Pakistan and Uganda. They discussed education in their respective nations and supporting the success of students. This day continued to be very interactive with youth sharing experiences, ideas, and discussing the way forward. It was now lunch time and time to take it easy.

The walk back to our campground was as challenging as always with the heat. One would almost prefer not to have clothes on because it was so hot here. As an African born, I am used to the heat, but this was just too much. Our VIP guest for the afternoon session was the Minister of Communication. After this session we went for another excursion to Ancient Chersonneus in the city of Sevastopol. Going for tours was one of my favourite things on this Forum because it was so well organized, filled with learning, and important facts about history. Our tour guide, Natasha, truly knew her history and there was a lot of history that she was put in charge of in our Crimea discovery. She would always say, "Stay close to me."

Because other teams also had their own tour guides. The day came to an end and it was time to head back to the camp. I was very grateful for such wonderful adventures full of young people with energy and being well taken care of by the organizers. The organizers were eight youths with many more volunteers who really knew what they were doing. For a young person like me, I felt really proud that such young people could put something together as wonderful, adventurous and well organized like this. Youths indeed are capable of doing anything when setting their mind to something. On our last day at the camp, August 19th, many were filled with a sense of gratitude and we got to appreciate the organizers and volunteers who we were under the wings of. This turned out to be about what transpire on this day, but first, let's conclude the events of August 15th and talk about the other days before we reach that emotional and fixed feelings day. The Forum from here kept on getting more electrifying with awesome excursions which we were honoured to go to and be a part of history.

The morning of August 16th started as always but it was in no way near the same as others. Each and every day was very unique filled with its own wonders, blessings and discoveries. We did not have any sessions that day, but all of our learnings took place at a very historic place called Yalta. When everyone was ready, we boarded the buses and began a journey which seemed like forever before reaching our destination. Sometimes we were offered bags filled with bread, apples, water and chocolates for the journey to excursions. We visited Livadia Palace where the US president, Franklin D Roosevelt, UK Prime Minister, Winston Churchill, and the Premier of Soviet Union, Joseph Stalin, had met in February of 1945 to talk about Europe and territories disputes. Natasha showed us around where the three men had met, the office, the lunch room, the place of negotiation and much more.

We took lots and lots of pictures and I had a sense of a feeling that I was a part of history. I remember at one point a girl with her parents calling to me requesting for a picture. And I said, "SURE." These kind of explorations don't just happen and many people spend a lot of money to come and see what we, the delegates, were being exposed to. I was very grateful to the Russian Government for such opportunities which I had never thought possible in my life. Before the Tavrida Forum, I had never even hear about such history and being present was even more awesome, a feeling like no other. The tour continued and our superiors had a magnificent surprise in store for us which put smiles all over our faces. We got back into the buses and drove to a nearby restaurant where we found nice tables, eating utensils and everyone started rejoicing. Donatus, Jerry, Denys and myself sat at one table.

The first course which was salad, followed by soup and the final surprise was the main course. We were even offered juice. I needed water and asked for the waiter and he brought bottles also for Donatus and Jerry. The next thing we noticed was a bill being handed to us and we started laughing because we had no idea that we would have to pay. We put our money together, paid for the water, and enjoyed it with pleasure because it was so hot. The restaurant was located at a very beautiful location with a nice view of the mountains and the black sea. I was full like never before since arriving at the Forum. At the camp the food would be the same almost all the time, but there was this one day when we were taken outside the camp for a real meal in what seemed like a military compound. When it came to the food that we were used to having every day, some delegates would say that it is military food and there's no argument there. The camp experience was great, but no one was a fan of the food. Oh by the way, our security at the camp was provided by the military and there was a base within the camp.

After our amazing lunch we were taken to the market to buy some souvenirs. We were even given the chance to buy wine for souvenirs for those interested but we would have to give them to our superiors until the end of the Forum when it would be handed back. One of the rules of the Forum was no alcohol allowed. Since we had been going to these excursions, I had been looking for a t-shirt which says Russia or Crimea on it but I was yet to find one. This was my mission when we arrived at the market. I looked around but had no success finding the t-shirt. We walked around and some people bought food, water, wines, body products and I bought batteries for my camera. The batteries which I brought with me had finished very quickly and I had come to the conclusion that it might be because of the hot weather.

Everyone finished their shopping and we met back at the parking lot where the buses were waiting for us. When I came out of the supermarket, three guys who looked very drunk were happy to see me and requested a picture but they did not have a camera and so I took a picture with mine. I love putting smiles on people's faces and make their day. One of the delegates, Denis, had bought watermelons which he gladly shared with everyone before boarding the buses. It was once again a long journey back to the camp and we arrived after 20:30 and relaxed in our tents while we waited for the evening entertainment which began around 21:30. The entertainment was sports on the stage and dancing. I did not wait for the entertainment to finish and went to rest in my tent. I spent awhile on my technology, went for an evening shower and was ready for some sleep.

Chapter 5: Shaping the Future

With only three days of the Forum remaining, the excitements continued and the feeling of coming to an end started kicking in. The night before, Caroline had approached some delegates about presenting topics of their choice because the theme of the morning session was 'Discover the World'. I was among the people who she approached and I responded with a cheerful 'YES'. This time my topic of choice was 'Lack of Youth Engagement in Society' and it was mainly focused in Africa but we tried to relate back to our respective communities globally. Other presented topics were: 'Education' (Latin America), 'Women Empowerment' (Asia),

'Loss of Youth Generation' (East Europe) and 'Regionalization' (Middle East).

This was our opportunity to once again talk about the issues which effected everyone and come up with solutions which would shape the future. When given the platform to introduce their topics, all the delegates brought their points across with passion and the desire to see things change. Just like the previous day, delegates chose which presentation to head to and they were rotating between the discussions. The room was very lively and most people made their voices heard by talking about the situations, causes, and finding better ways to move forward. Some of the things which were talked about in the 'Women Empowerment' discussions was; Education, Say No, Successful Women to Set Examples, Women legislation, Political Lobbying, Sharing traditional Work Space for Women and Moving Step by Step.

Some of the issues that came up for 'Lack of Youth Engagement in Society' were: Leaders holding onto Power, Lack of Awareness on youth issues, No Youth Policies, Lack of Education, and Individualism (self-interests). We then all agreed that the best way to shape the future is for the youths who are already active to share their vision and engage others. We also talked about lobbying for Youth Policies in governments and instructing youths so that they know their rights and responsibilities. Furthermore, there needs to be a Youth Parliament which will advocate for the issues affecting youths for the benefits of everyone. I felt very proud taking the leadership role and leading this great conversation which will also benefit me in my quest to get youths involved and playing key roles in societies. This is indeed a great way to kick off the morning session. We summarized up all the discussions and presented to the larger group once again. I closed my topic and we posed for a picture with loud cheers of 'AFRICA'. Most of the African delegates and others came running waiting to be included in the picture. This was a joyous moment with everyone feeling so energetic. We then had the opportunity to present the summary of our topics on stage.

The day continued on an exciting note when different sessions on Services and Delivering Happiness were presented. One of the quotes from Maya Angelou was showed on the screen, "I've learned that people will forget what you said, people will forget what you did, but people will never forget how you made them feel." The presentation on 'Service' was to encourage us to find meaning in the vision of a company and one which people will connect with. Some of the key points from the presentation on 'Delivering Happiness' were: Embrace and Drive Change, Create Fun and a Little Weirdness, Pursue Growth and Learning, Be Adventurous, Creative, and Open-Minded, Be Passionate and Determined and Be Humbled. This was a very interactive, fun, and helpful session. It is something which everyone could relate to because I believe we all want to be happy in life through the things that we do. This concluded the morning session and it was now lunch time. The weather was a little bit cooler because we were expecting a storm in the night and so the day was not very hot.

After lunch we visited The Khan's Palace (Hansaray) in Bakhchysarai which is considered to be an ancient Turkish city. We learned about things such as The Fountain of Tears which was created in 1764 and The Harem Building which was built in the 18th century. I love learning about history and I thanked the organizers of this Forum for making this Tavrida International Youth Forum worthwhile. I have never heard about this part of history but now I know a lot and have lots of pictures and diary entires filled with beautiful memories. These are the kinds of adventures which we live to tell about the fun and discoveries which took place. Just like yesterday, our organizers had once again prepared a stunning surprise which lit up everyone's faces. We had got into the buses and drove to a nearby restaurant and what we saw was just amazing, tables full of food already.

The restaurant was next to a different mountain while we enjoyed one of the best lunches since arriving at the Forum. This kind of food was certainly making up for the previous days and nobody was complaining, but loving every minute of it. There was salad, juice and a main course all ready for our pleasure. My weight was now coming back and my trouser was surely tight now. You could just see people's faces filled with joy because of such surprises and wishing it happened every day. It was time to head back to the camp and I had a good nap while in the bus because I was quite full. This journey back would mark our last excursion of the Forum and the next one would be while heading to the airport for takeoff and dismissal. When we arrived at the campgrounds we went for the afternoon session and we were addressed about preparation for an emergency and getting ready for the storm. We were instructed by our leaders to gather and move our belongings to the military compound where we had once gone for a beautiful lunch surprise. I miss those kind of surprises.

    We moved our stuff and we were taught that we might be woken up anytime during the night to move to a safer location which was in the halls where we held our sessions. The big tents of meeting places for each team were also brought down so as not to fly away during the storm. This was a very serious and nervous afternoon and we were prepared but no one can really be prepared for Mother Nature. As I sat down to write in my journal, I could see the worry and seriousness on people's faces. The feeling of unknown was not a pleasant one. For the rest of the afternoon we were given the free time in order to get ready for Global Village the next day. We were divided and it was decided that the presentations would be based on continents and not individually. People from Asia got together that afternoon to prepare and so did those from Europe, Americas, and

Africa. I had joined the African group and also said I would represent Canada. I tried to reach across to my fellow Canadian, Kayla, to join force and present together but she did not seem interested. Kayla was saying that she does not know what to present on, but I strongly persisted and to no success. My meeting with fellow Africans came to an end and we agreed on who will say something, play music and together we will all dance. Shortly after I was off to bed.

And then came August 18th, Global Village Day. The wind was very strong during the night and we were woken up by Denys around 7am to head to the session hall because it seemed like the storm was here. There was a bit of rain and plastic bags were offered to us for protection against getting wet. We made the journey to the halls where for the first time we would have our breakfast that morning. A movie was played and we sat quietly enjoying. The movie was based on the first Russian man on the Moon and it was very interested with subtitles. Our breakfast was during the movie and an announcement was made that people were needed to help to put back the big tents for team meeting location. It seemed as if the storm had forgiven us and it was just strong wind during the night.

I was among those delegates who had volunteered to go and help put back the tents. We headed back to the hall when we finished putting back the tents and we were ready for our morning session. Our session was on a bit more of Russian and Crimean history. Throughout the Forum, whenever a speaker would address us in Russian, our beautiful and amazing translator would help us understand. At times we would mentioned that she was doing such a great job and this encouraged her to continue. Sometimes she had difficulty but our cheers kept motivating her. After this session we had lunch and also went to get our belongings from where we had stored them because of the storm. I forgot who our VIP guest was for that afternoon but he spoke about Russian politics.

After the VIP guest we were given about an hour to prepare for Global Village and it was the most exciting and entertaining show which us, the delegates, had made happen. Our leaders provided flags and those who did not bring any could grab from there. All delegates were proudly waving their flags up in the air with enormous smiles on their faces and happy to represent where they come from. I believe altogether the International Delegates were over 50 and you could see flags such as: Brazil, US, China, Vitamin, Uganda, Hong Kong, India, Pakistan, Nigeria, Namibia, Canada, Spain, India, Russia, Somalia, Qatar, Ecuador, Palestine and much more. Delegates sang, performed traditional dances and the Africans were just as awesome as everybody else. All continents put a great show together and it was a very proud and emotional moments. My brother, Attaf, stood tall while the National Anthem of Palestine played, prayed for peace and everyone applauded when the Anthem finished. At this every moment, whether big or small, many nations came together and we all wished the world was as peaceful like this where everyone live together in harmony.

    This Forum had brought people from all walks of life and here we were giving each other big hugs, celebrating one another, and taking pictures with each other and our respective flags. I had probably the biggest smile on my face with a great sense of belonging, and the desire to continue my community involvement and connecting with fellow passionate youths from around the world. At this Forum I had utilize the experiences and knowledge I had gained throughout the years at other Youth Forum and also learned so much more. Just as I respected what my fellow delegates brought to the table, they also admired what I stood for, my contributions and the joyfulness that I brought to the camp. Even my Team 7 leaders, Denys and Nika, commented on how cheerful I was, always on my journal, and contributing to the team dynamic. This is my nature, the kind of person that I am. And my leaders had a wonderful surprise for me at the end of the closing ceremony the next day. I completely had no idea about the surprise but I was all along being the best Gerard that I could possibly be. You will have to continue reading until the end of the book in order to learn about the wonderful surprise I received and the beauty of staying true to yourself no matter the surroundings.

    The Global Village continued with more dancing, cheering and delegates embracing each other for the perfect show. The organizers had thanked us for bringing the energy and making the day such a success. I had proudly presented the Democratic Republic of the Congo with fellow Africans and Canada on the Americas side

(North and South America and Central). I was a man presenting different continents and I was delighted. I searched around to see where Kayla was and could not find her among the crowd. Astonishingly, it turned out she was sleeping during the whole experience. While other youths were proudly representing their nations and having a great time together, Kayla, was peaceful sleeping. I was not pleased with her actions when I found out later. We concluded our Global Village and got ready for dinner. The involvement with Global Village Day will forever live with me and every time I look at the pictures, my heart smiles along because it was such an important occasion.

After dinner, the evening's entertainment was comedy in Russian and I did not understand a thing. I just stood there and admired the show when I decided to go and rest in my tent before the show finished. At the campground I believe we were nearly almost 2000 youths. Sometimes we had sessions together with other delegates but mostly we would be by ourselves as International Delegates. The other groups I believe were Russians and we all had different themes but shared the same campground and interacted with each other sometimes.

You should have seen me trying to communicate with some girls who could not communicate in English. I was always entertaining and trying to make some gesture with my hands or different sounds. For example, I remember one day when we visited Bakhchisaray, some of us international Delegates shared the table with a Russian girl and the way I tried to communicate brought everyone to laugher. I had made the sound of a goat when I tried to say that the green on my plate is for goats. Another time we were showing each other IDs and I pulled mine out making the sound of a car in to order make the person understand that it is a Driver's Licence. These are just kinds of memories that one remembers when it is all set and done.

Chapter 6: Thank You. Well Wishes. Until We Meet Again

I could not believe that our time at the camp, with Tavrida, and all these incredible and passionate change-makers had come to an end. I did exchange contact information with many people and we added each other on Facebook so I had no doubt that I would be communicating with some of them when I get back to Canada. Since arriving at this Forum, this was the most emotional day of them all, the goodbyes. This morning I decided to skip the morning exercise and stay in the tent for a little more sleep and reflect on the past few days. One part of me was excited to go back home and spread the word about what I had learned in Crimea, the hospitality, and talk about the wonderful excursions we went to. Whereas, another part of me wanted to just stay here in the company of fellow youths and continue our time together. I had felt such a sense of belonging and connected so well with the delegates that I was not ready for the goodbyes. I left for a shower, ate breakfast and was ready for the morning session. Just as we had begun, this concluding morning session was also on history. A Historian Professor spoke about the history of Russia and Crimea and also mentioned some of the places we had visited during the tours. After that we then had a very interactive session where we talked about the future of Crimea and the changes that people want to see. Some key points such as: education, communication, young people, and resources were brought up.

This led us into lunch and before we could eat, we were instructed to pack our belongings, which most of us had already done, and put them in the buses. We also handed over our sleeping bags, our beds for the past few days. Many of the delegates including myself did not want all this to end. We were not ready to be apart from each other. Since arriving at the camp, we had become so close, learned from each other, and had so much fun together. The feeling of going our separate ways was one which I was not ready to accept yet. A great amount of me was saying, "I'm ready to go back and take on the world" and another part just wanted to stay a little bit longer. We helped one another with luggage carrying to the buses and returned for lunch. I believe almost all of our belongings were already packed anyway due to the preparation of the storm. Some of us just had to fold the sleeping bags and hand them to our leaders with gratitude.

  Speaking of our leaders, Denys and Nika from Team 7, were just amazing throughout the Forum. Whether it was waking us up, calling for food, getting ready for the sessions, or team meetings, these two great people did an awesome job. They took the time to make sure everyone was accounted for, communicate to the delegates about the helpful information, and were always present when needed. There were times when things seemed overwhelming, but they dealt with every situation accordingly and we finished the Forum with great love and respect for each other. After lunch our afternoon session was led by VIPs who were the authorities of Crimea. The Governor had come with his Minister of Tourism, Foreign Minister and some military who were given awards right before our very own eyes because of their work during the referendum and keeping the peace.

Before our respective guest even spoke, a video was shown on the big screen about the Crimea Referendum, how it was announced and when President Vladimir Putin signed the papers. People were very emotional during the whole process and when the video finished, all the delegates applauded. This was also among the sessions which we were mixed with our delegates. The hall was so full and people were listening very carefully. Questions were always taken at the end, but I remember the Deputy Minister of Education taking his questions before hand. There were lot of questions from the floor such as, business opportunities, youth projects, and whether citizens of Crimea were happy to be part of Russia. This was a very interactive and interesting session filled with laughers. The session finished and we were given 10 minutes break before we started another session on Crimea.

During the walking around I remember my brother Yagouba, from Guinea, and myself running into Sergey Aksenov, the Governor of Crimea. We requested a picture and his securities were trying to protect him but he granted our request and we asked his security to even take the pictures with our phones. We then joined the other session based on Crimea conversation and the role that the media played internationally. I recall a comment of the journalists saying that some journalist at times are the kind who go around looking for stories and always have negative things to say about every situation. Almost all delegates applauded because we had lot of journalists among us and one of them was Aleksey, from Latvia and delegate from Team 7. Aleksey was also the one who had helped put together such an interesting conversation. He was a gentleman who I loved, respected, and communicated well with as fellow delegate of Team 7.

After the short session on Crimea, it was now time to thank all of our amazing volunteers which followed by thanking the organizers. This was yet another session time and a sad reminder that we were beginning to say our farewells already. When the volunteers were called up in the front to be awarded with certificates, the hall which we were in came much alive because all the delegates were shouting loud for their leaders. These great and dedicated young people had voluntarily agreed to supervise and help us with our Tavrida experience. When they called out the name of Team 7 leaders, Denys and Nika, I stood up and screamed so loud with a sense of gratitude. I was very grateful to all the volunteers, organizers, delegates, security, evening entertainments, the tours, and much more which made the whole experience worthwhile that I was not yet ready to say goodbye to these incredible people.

Caroline then led us by showing an inspiring video and gave us about three minutes to go around the room to give hugs and tell fellow delegates whatever we wanted. This was a great opportunity to further appreciate each other. This moment almost brought me to tears. It was now time for dinner and after that our last evening entertainment, the closing ceremony. Do you remember that Anthem, Tavrida? It was almost played every morning and could hear it while still sleeping in the tent. Even though I did not understand anything, I fell in love with that song and the way I would sing along brought joy to fellow delegates. Not sure whether they were laughing with me or at me, either way, I could not hold back I felt whenever that song came on. I was like, TAVRIDA… TAVRIDA!!!

The closing ceremony was one like I had never seen before. It started with a lot of performances and the International Delegates got to go up on the stage with their respective flags and wave them like never before. We screamed and shouted with great joy and those on the ground responded with the same expressions. After this, the leaders then gathered one representative from each team and we had no idea what was going on. It turned out it was time for that wonderful surprise which I had spoken off. We proudly went back up on the stage with our flags and when we came down, our leaders handed us awards for our contributions and making the Forum a success. I had no idea that something like this lay ahead and I was very grateful to be the only one to receive from Team 7 with almost 20 amazing youths.

With over 50 countries being represented and over 120 youths from all corners of the world, not to mention the thousands of

Russian delegates among us, I was honoured and proud to have been part of the first ever Tavrida International Youth Forum. The closing ceremony which was filled with performances followed by 5 minutes worth of fireworks continued with very energetic youths. Many delegates including myself still had our flags and I was proudly waving the Canadian flag up high. The party went on past 00:00 when we welcomed August 20th and started heading to the buses for our journey to the airport in Simferopol. We left our fellow Russian delegates continuing with the ceremony because most of them were to leave during the day on August 20th. You could hear loud cheers and fellow youths waving goodbyes as we headed to board the buses. I looked back with a great sense of gratitude and waved goodbye to the youths who had not only become friends, but also family.

During the Forum, I had also met many delegates from Crimea, including our very own leader, Denys. The journey to the airport was very silent with everyone resting and feeling sad about the departing. Some of the leaders, including ours, had stayed behind and would depart during the day. We said emotional farewells and I thanked them for everything and their dedication to making this Forum and the experience worthwhile. Denys had told me that he would surly love to read my journal and I promised him that he would surely read it. Also Egor, the Press Secretary of the Forum and one of the organizers had shown great interests and was even the one who first mentioned the idea that I should write a book about Tavrida. Many people who saw or knew that I had kept a journal raised their interests and inspired me to continue writing and turn it into something bigger upon my arrival to Canada. We arrived at the airport in Simferopol around 3am, checked in our bags, and received our boarding passes.

    Our flight left shorting after 4am and you could see the tiredness from people's body languages or maybe it was the sadness of leaving each other? We had felt such a great sense of security around each other and we would surly remember and treasure our time together at the campgrounds, the swimming days, the excursions, the sessions and the fun. Our plane landed in Moscow at the same airport, Sheremetievo, when it was around 7am. This is where, for us International Delegates, our farewells and well wishes for each other really began. We patiently waited for our luggage while hugging and saying our goodbyes. Soon we all had our belongings and those who were to take the train to their final destination within Russia left. Many others went back to the hotel because they will be departing for the homeland tomorrow or the next day. And as for me, my flight was to leave from the same airport heading to JFK. While fellow delegates were exiting the airport, I felt tears in my eyes and wanted to follow them. I had become so close to so many of them and I will miss them greatly. I watched as they exited the airport and I stayed in waiting for my flight which was to leave at 12pm.

    A part of me had the biggest smile on my face for having lived through the past few days with these awesome International Delegates, whereas, another part of me wanted the experience to continue. I had learned a lot from the speakers, the VIP guests, the organizers, the leaders, from fellow delegates and I sensed that I was indeed ready to take on the world and continue with my involvement with young people. Whether it was talking about the food, the heat, people wishing for more meat, the worries, or the joyous days, we were all together as one wishing and ready to shape the future.

Chapter 7: Contributions from Fellow Delegates

TAKE HOME REFLECTION ON OUR VISIT TO SEVASTOPOL. (TAVRIDA 2014)

My dear participants of the TAVRIDA 2014 and indeed global viable youths of today, I humbly greet you all. I thanked the organizers of TAVRIDA International youth forum who gave me the privilege to be part of the delegates of this year's event in the Crimea region of Sevastopol Russian. It was an awesome experience because the program was an eye opener to so many, empowering and educationally enriching to mention a few.

It was during this program, that opportunity was created for us to share our passion on (THE IMPACT I DARE TO MAKE) and I came up with what disturbs me most: A TOPIC TITLLED – THE THREAT TO THE GLOBAL ENVIRONMENT. The discussion on this topic was narrowed down to our behaviour towards the environment. However, many may have forgotten about this but due to the fact that it gives me serious concern, I am writing here as a take home reflection to all of us and every other person who is reading this right now. I will make our discussion here as brief and precise as possible.

We are the youths of today with hopes, dreams and the future belongs to us. We have the mandate to protect our environment at all cost so that we can live on it. Do you agree? As for me, the answer is "Yes, I do". Then, what can we do to protect the environment or do you think there is no threat to it? Let me jog your memory a little bit;-

When we talk about environment, it implies all the external factors living and non-living, material and non-material which surrounds man. In the modern concept, it includes not only the water, air and soil that form our environment but also the social and economic conditions under which we live. This means that customs, culture, habits, income, occupation, religion among others are factors of consideration on environmental degradation.

Industrial growth has given rise to the problem of environmental pollution by industrial wastes.

Advances in nuclear technology have produced the problem of radioactive pollution of the environment.

Fast urbanization all over the world is bringing profound social and environmental changes. Climate change which is causing the oceans to warm, ozone layer deflection, deforestation etc. are global issues of today.

You will agree with me that a combined multi-disciplinary programme of action is needed to achieve healthy positive result on our behaviour to the environment. The time has come to depend not only on the legal action, which are often only minimal and temporary, and instead requires constant vigilance to assure compliance.

Therefore, emphasis has to change and be placed on the education of people towards voluntary acceptance of behavioural constraints rather than relying on the threat of legal and police actions common to our various communities. We must change our direction to an educational approach in order to achieve maximum result.

Finally, do not forget that your actions and mine to the environment are important because it determines what becomes of the environment we live in today. Whatever we give, we shall receive. Let us protect our environment and be conscious of our behaviour to the environment. Spread the good news.

THANKS YOU. DONATUS ANAYO OKPARA.

TAVRIDA 2014

My whole TAVRIDA experience can be summed up in one word: amazing! I have never been to any event that has had such a lasting impact. Even when we had all returned home, none of us could really believe it was over; none of us wanted it to be over. It seemed like it took forever to get my telex number. I wasn't sure if I was going to be able to get my visa in time. I had even talked myself into thinking I wasn't going to make it. It was almost too crazy to think I would be able to go to Russia and Crimea. When the plane took off from San Francisco, I finally let myself relax. Nothing I imagined prepared me for my stay and at the end I was surprised to find I didn't want to go home. Moscow and Crimea were beautiful and nothing like what I had imagined. TAVRIDA was nothing like what I had imagined either.

The forum brought people together in ordinary yet profound ways that formed bonds between the international participants. It wasn't any one thing, but the accumulation of the many big and small things we did every day. We ate meals, attended presentations, toured, and basically did everything together. Our days were planned, but we still found times of wonderful spontaneity. We swam and walked and talked and danced and most of all laughed together. As I waited at the airport to go back to the US, I stuffed down an urge to cry. It was hard to say goodbye, to leave Russia, to let go of my friends, to go back to my home. I was different somehow and the thought of home didn't have the same pull. As I was replaying the past days in my mind, I realized I still had Rubles in my pocket. I pulled them out and counted them. Wonderful! I have enough to pay for an Aeroexpress, a metro ticket, and a snack so now I know I will be able to go back to Russia.

ELISABETH TSITOURA

Reflection. Hopes

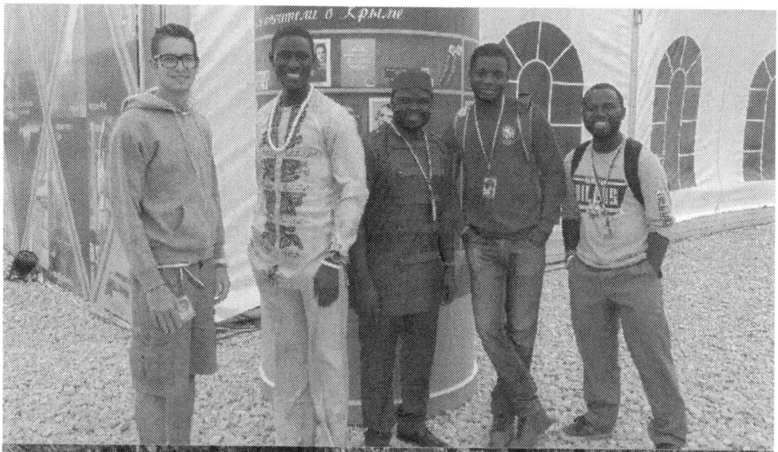

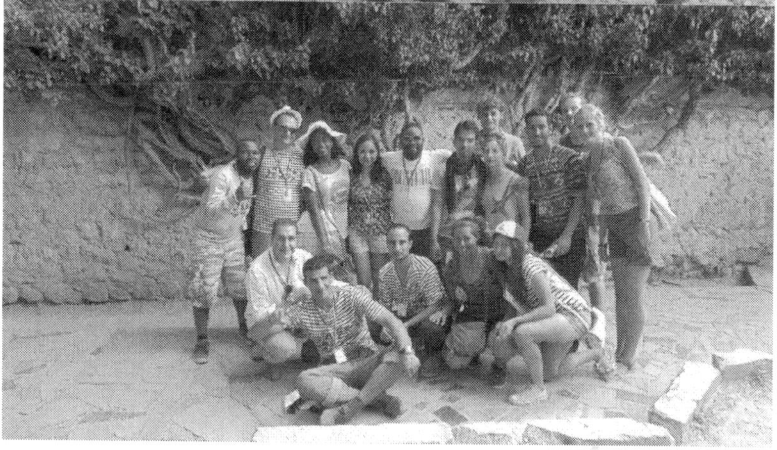

The first two above pictures are that of Team 7 leaders, Denys and Nika. I had so much admiration for Denys and Nika and I loved every moment that I was under their guidance. The other pictures are just a few from thousands of the awesome International Delegates. I truly wish I could include all pictures with their own personal story, but those memories will forever live with me. I am grateful and appreciated everything that each delegate brought to the Forum and I was inspired by their actions. I learned a lot from this experience and the need for a better world was re-established and that the work has just begun. I was honoured to get a taste of the rich Russian history, language, culture and be surrounded by awesome Russian youths who also shared the desire for a better world.

To the Russian Government, thank you so much for opening your borders and allowing the International Youths to be part of this unforgettable and life changing experience. To the organizer team of Tavrida and the Federal Agency on Youth Affairs of Russian Federation, I was truly honoured to take part in the Forum and thanks for selecting me among the many who applied. Thank you for the wonderful and well put together Forum. Thank you for the security, excursions, sessions, the surprises, and thank you for allowing every delegates to bring their own personality in order to make the Forum a success.

To my fellow International Delegates, thank you for contributing to my knowledge of youth work and it was great hearing about some of the projects that you have going on. And to fellow Local Delegations from Crimea and general Russia, thank you for your hospitality and giving me personal moments to remember when I couldn't communicate with some of you due to language barrier. Thank you to the bus drivers, the amazing tour guides, the police escorts and thank you to everyone who was behind the scene to ensure we are having the best time of our lives.

Hopes

Vision: To positively lead change and be a contributing member of society at home and around the world. This vision is among the many driving forces in everything that I do. Currently I am in the BBA Management at NAIT with the hope of completing in April of 2016. I am also registered in online classes at Lakeland College in their Certificate Development program. The dream, goal and desire is to work across the globe in lending my voice and expertise to the much needed people. I have interests in Leadership, Humanitarian, Business, Human Rights, and Good Governance.

I would like to give a huge appreciation to my dear family for their continuous support and allowing me to be the best that I can be while inspiring and transforming the lives of others. I think it is safe to say that my mom, Yvonne Rehema, has been my biggest support, motivator, and inspiration through everything I do. She is always there for advice and I am grateful to the Lord for having her in my life. She is continuously encouraging me to achieve and be the best.

My desire and life calling is to be there for those less fortunate and speak for the voiceless whenever possible. I am a Youth & Child Activist and I am never shy to speak when I notice injustice happening. In the famous words of Martin Luther King Jr. "Injustice anywhere is a threat to justice everywhere." As a youth myself, I want to continue working with young people whether in the community or globally in order to find solutions to the issues that affect us all.

Born in 1990 in Uvira, Democratic Republic of the Congo (DRC), I spent my childhood as a Refugee in Refugee Camps and lived in Cape Town, South Africa for about 6 years. Since arriving in Canada in 2008 under the Refugee Status sponsored by the Canadian Government, I have strived for the best that life has to offer. With no High School background, I registered in NorQuest College's English program called Youth in Transition and went about getting my High School Equivalent Education in order to register in the Business Administration program at NAIT in 2012. I have completed my Diploma and I am now working toward a Bachelor's Degree in Management.

Throughout the years, I have been honoured and very blessed to have had opportunities to travel around the world on Youth Missions, work on community projects, advocate for students, volunteer, and much more. I am very grateful to all of those who have played a huge role in my life whether it was teachers, fellow youths, society, mentors, family or friends. This book is dedicate to all of you, and most importantly, is dedicate to my wonderful MOTHER who continues to be my rock and my everything with unconditional love.

Made in the USA
Charleston, SC
03 January 2015